*In loving memory
of Blanche Wilson and Phyllis Tickle*

Contents

Contents

1

Introduction

God Be in My Head, I'll wager, is the best old prayer you never heard of. If you're old-prayer savvy, you might know it as the Sarum Prayer. You may know it as a hymn—an excellent way to deliver a prayer. It's the sort of prayer you can take with you through the day (think Lord's Prayer, Serenity Prayer, the Jesus Prayer, and the Prayer of St. Francis). Like so many great prayers, the Sarum Prayer covers our moment-by-moment living and our eventual dying—a full-spectrum prayer.

About that name, Sarum: it comes from a liturgical rite dated as early as 1527 (so it likely appeared much earlier) associated with a region in England called Sarum or Old Sarum (modern day Salisbury). There were and are many different liturgical rites—Latin, Byzantine, Coptic, etc.—and the Sarum Rite is one that was overshadowed and partly absorbed into more well-known ones, such as we have in the Book of Common Prayer or the Latin Missal. You don't need to know or care about all that in order to use the Sarum Prayer, which is also known by a simpler name, taken from its opening line, "God be in my head."

Yes, five simple and elegant lines:

> *God be in my head–and in my understanding*
> *God be in my eyes–and in my looking*
> *God be in my mouth–and in my speaking*
> *God be in my heart–and in my thinking*
> *God be at my end–and at my departing.*

What's not to like about this prayer? I can't think of anything.

It's *short*. At five lines—shorter than the Lord's Prayer—it expresses a lot with a little.

It's *old*. This prayer was composed in a time when words weren't as profuse as they are today, expressing ways of seeing ourselves (like thinking with our hearts) that nudge us into new-for-us ways of perceiving God.

It's *physical*. The prayer is focused on four faculties associated with four parts of the body, and a final line that reminds us of a key aspect of our current embodied existence: mortality.

It's *memorable*. Just recall the following pairs in descending anatomical order: head-understanding, eyes-looking, mouth-speaking, heart-thinking (followed by end-departing) and you've got it.

It's *genderless*. No "he" for God, no "she" for God (no neuter "it," either, for that matter), just God.

It's *mystical*. Because of the prayer's focus on our bodies (temples, after all, of the Spirit), the prayer is also mystical, focused on a God who dwells in us.

> *God be in my head–and in my understanding*
> *God be in my eyes–and in my looking*
> *God be in my mouth–and in my speaking*
> *God be in my heart–and in my thinking*
> *God be at my end–and at my departing.*

This guide offers forty short meditations to be used over forty days. Of course, you can read it in a single sitting or two if you prefer, but easy does it, one day at a time, may be a more fruitful approach. That way you can let this gem of a prayer work its way into your—well—head, eyes, mouth, heart, and make you a little less apprehensive about your own mortality.

You notice: forty days—the length of the season of Lent—six and a half weeks, not counting Sundays (because everyone needs a break once a week). Whether you use it for Lent or not, forty days happens to correspond to what psychologists regard as a good length of time to start a new habit. After forty days (give or take) of trying something new—a process that always takes a little effort—things become habitual, easier, more natural, an almost effortless part of our life. In other words, a little focused attention over the course of forty days will likely result in this prayer slipping into you for easy and ready access as needed. It could become one of those things that gently shapes your soul.

And what a lovely, intriguing, even powerful prayer to shape us!

> God be in my head–and in my understanding
> God be in my eyes–and in my looking
> God be in my mouth–and in my speaking
> God be in my heart–and in my thinking
> God be at my end–and at my departing.

If we're to spend a brief part of forty days together, you might appreciate knowing some of the assumptions I make, born of many of years of praying, trying to pray, and helping people who are trying to pray. It turns out I have some opinions about this whole enterprise that have informed this guide.

First, I assume that many of us might also have a strong sense of liking certain prayers (and ways of praying) and disliking others. Which is to say you probably have an aesthetic sense about prayers—thoughts and feelings about what you like and dislike in a prayer, much as we do with music and art. I assume that some readers may have pretty defined opinions about what kinds of prayers are better or worse than others—a sense of agreement or disagreement over the content of certain prayers. Because we don't just pray prayers, we think about the prayers we pray. All that seems very normal, very like us.

Beneath the way that we may or may not assess prayers, I also assume that many of us, most of us, all but a very few of us (and I wonder about them) feel a great deal of private insecurity about our praying—or maybe more to the point, about how well or whether we are able to connect with God in and with our praying. So I also assume there's a voice in your head as in mine, speaking more or less insistently, saying something like, "What's the point of all this anyway?" No matter how deeply committed we are to our spiritual path, there's a part of us that feels very much like an agnostic feels, or an atheist for that matter.

I think a lot of this sense of insecurity about praying is the product of our culture and not just our own doing. We live in an era deeply shaped by the pursuit of mastery, of technological wizardry and scientific achievements that were hard to imagine not so long ago. Most of us are much less involved with nature, spend less time outdoors—other than whizzing through relatively barren landscapes in our various high-speed transit modes. All of this makes us much less confident, or skilled even, in discerning realities that most other people in most other eras of human history simply took for granted. We don't assume, like so many of our ancestors did, that the world is shot-through with divinity; that humans are embodied spirits (or inspirited bodies); and that God is as near as our next breath—and *of course* divine presence would inhabit us, work through us, and wink at us from time to time through the world around us.

Most of us may like the sound of all that, but we haven't been pickled in a society, a culture, a social world, that takes it for granted anymore. It's left us all a bit lacking in confidence to proceed.

So we question ourselves incessantly, and wonder if we're "doing it right" when it comes to praying, critically evaluating ourselves, and assuming everyone gets it better than we do. Just in case you're wondering, that goes for most clergy I know too, including the ones who are really into God and praying and the rest.

All to say, I'm trying to take that reality into account in these meditations—to go gently, and proceed, at times indirectly, to break things down into manageable bits, to look at things from different angles, and to communicate a sense that we're all in this together.

I'm also happy to report that most people don't need to learn how to be more spiritual, they just need to relax enough (and slow down enough) to notice how spiritual they can't help being—given the sort of world we live in, so obviously affected by powerful realities that transcend what we can capture or master or explain away. Along those lines, as the undisputed expert on your own praying—what works, what doesn't—take the sparing suggestions about method (praying a line ten times over, for example) as just that: suggestions. If they don't resonate, pass them by without a second thought.

So let's get started. Before diving right into the first line of the prayer, let's begin with four short meditations on the Sarum Prayer as a whole—circling around the prayer a bit, the way my old golden retriever used to circle a few times before lying down.

2

Opening Reflections on the Sarum Prayer

Day 1
on the point of prayer in the first place

Prayer is about improving our conscious contact with God, a phrase from Step 11 of the twelve steps of Alcoholics Anonymous (AA):

> Step 11: Sought through prayer and meditation to improve our conscious contact with God as we understood Him, praying only for knowledge of His will for us and the power to carry that out.[1]

Like so much about AA, "improving our conscious contact with God" is a phrase loaded with time-tested and hard-fought wisdom. It suggests we have some agency; there are things we can do to improve our conscious contact with God. But it also implies that contact with God is more mysterious than our limited brains could possibly be conscious of at any given time. We may, in fact, be in contact with God *all the time*. The conscious contact part may simply be a matter of relaxing into something that's been there all along, like dipping our canoe paddle into a river that just keeps rolling along with or without our conscious contact.

Practical program that it is, AA offers a handful of prayers that have helped its members. They are generally short, to the point, and memorable.

The Sarum Prayer isn't part of the AA lineup, but it could be. Take a moment and try it on for size.

God be in my head—and in my understanding
God be in my eyes—and in my looking
God be in my mouth—and in my speaking
God be in my heart—and in my thinking
God be at my end—and at my departing.

Day 2
on the value of keeping a few set prayers handy

Of course we can make up prayers on the spot and do all the time—prayers like "Help" or "Let me get this job" or "You've got to be kidding me!"—but it also helps to have a few set prayers handy that have stood the test of time; prayers that remain in circulation because they work for enough people. These prayers are the winners of a fitness competition—like our genes, for example.

We're alive and old enough to read (or be read to) because we've all been fortunate enough to inherit genes that make life possible. We are a real biological success story in fact and so are all of our direct ancestors. Prayers go through a similar sorting process. Of all the prayers uttered or written down, only a relative few have survived for our use because enough people found them helpful for improving conscious contact with God.

We could do worse than to memorize a handful of such prayers to deploy when needed. Like the password for our smartphones, we don't want to have to look up a prayer when the need strikes.

This is a good one, the Sarum Prayer:

God be in my head–and in my understanding
God be in my eyes–and in my looking
God be in my mouth–and in my speaking
God be in my heart–and in my thinking
God be at my end–and at my departing.

Day 3
on the value of very old prayers

There's an eatery near my home called The Beaver Trap, specializing in *poutine*—French fries smothered in gravy and cheese curds, stuff that will kill you faster than fries alone. The sign says, "Loading fries since 2009." That's a long time ago! . . . if you're seven.

In the Sarum Prayer, we join voices that go back many centuries. Life in that time wasn't much different than when our forebears switched from hunter-gathering to farming 10,000 years earlier, give or take a millennium. Infant mortality was high, global population less than 500 million. People weren't into leveraging the Internet, plastic surgery, robotics, or artificial intelligence. They were in touch with their unadorned and essential humanity, which is with us today beneath all the sophisticated accoutrements of our time.

How we express ourselves is constrained by our culture. My parents didn't grow up hearing their parents tell them "I love you," a cultural constraint. I think they were missing something. Just as we're missing things their culture allowed, like going through the day without being exposed to 4,000 ads.

Our hearts are bigger than the culture of any particular era, including our own. It helps to have old-old prayers spoken from a very different time zone to express things that our time doesn't recognize or emphasize. It's like scratching an itch in the middle of your back that your contemporary culture can't reach.

Settle in to this old, old prayer, the Sarum Prayer.

God be in my head—and in my understanding
God be in my eyes—and in my looking
God be in my mouth—and in my speaking
God be in my heart—and in my thinking
God be at my end—and at my departing.

Day 4
on prayer as a bodily function

The theme of the Sarum Prayer is *God be in my body*. We'd normally say *God be in my spirit*—meaning some ethereal/non-material expression of us that may or may not exist. This prayer is different—more physical, more fleshy, more body-centered.

> God be in my head
> God be in my eyes
> God be in my mouth
> God be in my heart (meaning the thing
>   that beats in our chest)

What kind of God is this? Not a standard-issue one. When the book of Genesis was compiled (around 500 BCE) there was a common conception that God wouldn't directly create heaven-earth, because physical matter was too profane. So people imagined less and less concentrated versions of the divine called "demi-urges" that emanated from the pure divine. The one furthest out from God, the most diluted emanation of deity, did the dirty work of creating. This prayer, by contrast, reflects the significance of the incarnation—God inhabited human flesh in Jesus of Nazareth. The "big deal" of this isn't, Jesus is amazing! The big deal is that the God revealed in Jesus is at home in human flesh.

Which means such a God could be at home in us.

To appreciate how physical this prayer is, you might try touching your head for the first line, near your eyes for the second, your mouth for the third, your chest for the fourth, then holding both hands open for the final line of the prayer.

Let us pray,

> *God be in my head–and in my understanding*
> *God be in my eyes–and in my looking*
> *God be in my mouth–and in my speaking*
> *God be in my heart–and in my thinking*
> *God be at my end–and at my departing.*

3

God be in my head—
and in my understanding

Day 5

on getting acquainted with the first line of the Sarum Prayer

Consider how our prayer is structured: each line begins with the body part (head, eyes, etc.), followed by a corresponding function (understanding, looking, etc.). The effect of God's presence in our bodies is to facilitate, shape, and influence these functions.

The structure of the prayer is suited to meditative use. We can slow the prayer down by tying the first phrase of each line to the in-breath and the second phrase of each line to the out-breath (in-breath: "God be in my head"; out-breath: "and in my understanding").

This week, as you use the Sarum Prayer, put a little extra focus on the first line. You might take a few minutes with the prayer (in the morning, say). During this time, repeat the first line ten times before moving on to the rest of the prayer. Like this (italics indicates in-breath, regular font indicates out-breath):

***God be in my head**–and in my understanding* (x10)
God be in my eyes–and in my looking
God be in my mouth–and in my speaking
God be in my heart–and in my thinking
God be at my end–and at my departing.

Remember that first line, in particular, and call it to mind during the day (even if it's only once or twice):

God be in my head–and in my understanding

This is a simple meditative format you can use for each line, a week at a time for the next five weeks.

Day 6
on the lovely gift of understanding

We might think the highest function of our head-power is mental mastery, dominating various realms by knowledge. We spend the first three or four decades of life in pursuit of some form of mastery—getting good at something. Often that involves mental mastery. In many fields, it takes a long time to develop mental mastery.

In the Sarum Prayer, we're asking for the divine presence in our heads to foster *understanding*, different than mastery.

Mental mastery could be thought of as *over*standing rather than *under*standing.

Understanding calls for a different set of skills.

Think for a moment what a wonderful thing it is to be understood by someone.

Imagine that your mother is a doctor and her father was a doctor and she's always wanted you to be a doctor because it was so fulfilling for her to be a doctor. You've done well in college, aced the MCAT, and now you've been accepted by a top medical school. But you're not nearly as excited as your mother is and it gets you doing some soul-searching.

You realize (or finally admit to yourself) that this is your mother's dream for your life and you have a different one.

So you sit down to tell her that you're not excited about being a doctor, but you are excited about finding out what you really want to do with your life. In that moment, your mom realizes that what she really wants for you is a fulfilling life whatever that means for you. Then she opens her heart to listen . . . asking questions about what interests you, what your hopes and dreams are. You're able to pour out your heart and it feels like the first adult-to-adult conversation you've ever had with your mother. That's what it feels like to be understood—a powerful form of love.

As you go through your day today, use this prayer to help you understand someone as you would want to be understood.

God be in my head–and in my understanding (x10)
God be in my eyes–and in my looking
God be in my mouth–and in my speaking
God be in my heart–and in my thinking
God be at my end–and at my departing.

Day 7
on the humility and curiosity required by understanding

Understanding starts with humility—knowing that we don't know something and desiring to know it better. That's the genius of the discipline of science. A scientist is interested, not in what is already known, but in what is still unknown.

In the early days, a disciple would literally sit at the feet of a rabbi. This humble posture would signal interest, curiosity, and readiness to learn.

Curiosity implies attentiveness, alertness, and openness to whatever it is that isn't yet known—all crucial for gaining understanding.

Let's say your friend, or close coworker has a bit of a blind spot. You see something they don't. How you wish they would open up and give you a chance to explain your point of view. Wouldn't it be the most welcome thing if they gave you an honest hearing, asking only non-defensive questions for clarification—just like the marriage counselors coach their clients to do? They might even go the full distance of active listening and say, "I think I understand better now, but let me say it in my own words to see if I've got it right. You tell me." In the end, whether or not they eventually *agree* with you isn't as important as the work they put into *understanding* you. You would only grow in your affection, respect, and admiration for them. It would be as though God had been at work in them.

Today, look for an opportunity to make that kind of impression on someone nearby.

Let us pray,

> **God be in my head**–and in my understanding (x10)
> *God be in my eyes*–and in my looking
> *God be in my mouth*–and in my speaking
> *God be in my heart*–and in my thinking
> *God be at my end*–and at my departing.

Day 8
on what a bold prayer this really is

Consider how you've gained understanding over the course of your life. As a child, you thought one thing, but as an adult, you think another. Why? Because your perspective, your point of view, your vantage point changed.

To ask God for understanding is to ask for the view from a different vantage point than our own. To ask God for understanding is to be willing to think outside whatever box our head may be in: *For my thoughts are not your thoughts*, the Lord reminds us.

So, this is a big deal, asking God to be in our heads and in our understanding. It's a nervy thing to ask, and, when answered, may be unnerving. It's tantamount to asking God to change our minds, and who in their normal mind wants their mind to be changed, attached as we are to our long-standing opinions? Unless you've tasted what James Alison calls "The Joy of Being Wrong."

So much of our anxious striving goes into the project called "being right." In this mode, we become hard on ourselves and hard on others. Or as Jesus said, "Judge not, lest you be judged." Once we've discovered that this effort to be right can backfire, once we realize we've been wrong about something, we relax and take ourselves a little less seriously. And that can become a joyful experience.

So "God be in my head—and in my understanding" isn't some namby-pamby sentiment one might find in a run-of-the-mill inspirational greeting card. It's a bold prayer, the results of which, even if slow-fizz in their emerging, can be startling.

Let us, then, muster our courage to pray,

> **God be in my head–and in my understanding** (x10)
> *God be in my eyes–and in my looking*
> *God be in my mouth–and in my speaking*
> *God be in my heart–and in my thinking*
> *God be at my end–and at my departing.*

Day 9
on an open theory of mind

Tanya Luhrmann is a professor of anthropology at Stanford University who has studied people who think they experience God. Luhrmann says such people have a different "theory of mind" (or theory of how the mind works) than modern culture's prevailing "theory of mind." Whereas our prevailing theory of mind is naturalistic—that is, subject only to the influences of the natural world, including our own bodies—those who are open to experiencing God adopt a theory of the mind as semi-permeable to divine (or other spiritual) influences. Our thoughts may be inspired, shaped, triggered, informed, by divine energy and such thoughts may easily co-mingle with our own thoughts— all inside our head. Reassuringly, Luhrmann's research suggests that people who experience God (or think they do, at least) can be quite mentally healthy—that this mental experience is qualitatively different than say the experience of hearing voices as a symptom of psychosis.

To pray *God be in my head—and in my understanding* is to venture into an open theory of the mind. It is to entertain the possibility that we humans may be subject to divine influence—an influence that could affect, especially, our understanding, our perceptions, our making sense of things.

Have you ever had thoughts, feelings, impressions, mental images (while waking, sleeping, or daydreaming) that seem to be more loving, kind, compassionate, or wise than you are, left to your own devices? That's what we're talking about.

This very old prayer comes from an era when almost everyone had an open theory of mind. In fact, it would be difficult to find someone who didn't think their thoughts, feelings, inner impressions, and moods could be affected by divine influences. The reassurance of a professor of anthropology from an elite institution like Stanford wouldn't be needed.

Who's to say this older wisdom—a wisdom that welcomes and expects a little divine influence every so often—isn't a wisdom that corresponds to some aspects of reality that our modern, technological wisdom simply miss out on?

Let us pray then, with an open mind,

> **God be in my head**–and in my understanding (x10)
> God be in my eyes and in my looking
> God be in my mouth–and in my speaking
> God be in my heart–and in my thinking
> God be at my end–and at my departing.

Day 10
on sharing God's delight in understanding

So far, we've used examples of interpersonal understanding to consider how the divine presence in our heads might foster understanding as a form of love. The God to whom we pray a prayer like this is one who delights in the practice of understanding in whatever realm it functions. This is a God who creates *in* freedom (nothing compels God to create) but who also creates *for* freedom. In Genesis 1, God speaks things into being, beholds or sees what has been created, and only then does God declare it good. It's as though God is waiting for the creation to reveal itself and then responds to that revelation. The creation is free to be itself, related to God, but also distinct or separate from God. All of this is implicit in the words, "And God saw that it was good." Art Professor Jorella Andrews calls this "Showing Off."

When we are attentive to and curious about the world around us (plants, other creatures, the weather, how traffic flows, how a different language works, what makes music beautiful), and in that process of discovery gain understanding, we are participating with a God who relates to the creation in the same way. The delight that we experience is shared delight with God.

The next time you experience the kick of discovering how something works (say, you open that leaking toilet tank and figure out what the problem is and how to fix it), consider the possibility that your feeling of delight is a feeling that puts you into conscious contact with God.

Such a thing could intensify the simple pleasures.

In pursuit of joy, that fruit of the Spirit, let us pray,

> **God be in my head**–and in my understanding (x10)
> *God be in my eyes*–and in my looking
> *God be in my mouth*–and in my speaking
> *God be in my heart*–and in my thinking
> *God be at my end*–and at my departing.

4

※

God be in my eyes—
and in my looking

Day 11
on praying with our eyes open

God be in my eyes–and in my looking

The invitation to "close our eyes" to pray doesn't reflect spiritual wisdom so much as social convention. Many of our Jewish friends, for example, pray with open eyes.

I've heard it said we close our eyes to pray in order to reduce distraction, but sometimes things inside our head are as distracting as things outside. For this week, why not mix it up a little? Try praying "God be in my eyes—and in my looking" with your eyes open. It may help you be *less* distracted.

I tried this when I first developed chronic tinnitus (ringing in the ears). At first, when it doesn't go away (as ringing in the ears normally does), it can be quite annoying and you have to normalize to it—let it recede into the background. Paying attention to the ringing—that just makes it worse. At first, when I closed my eyes to pray with the tinnitus ringing away, it wasn't fun at all. So I prayed with eyes open. Much better.

You can try praying while looking at a burning candle, or a plant in your living room, or the trees outside your window. As your mind wanders (as minds are prone to do), gently return your focus to the words of the prayer . . . and whatever it is you're looking at.

Using the concrete language of anthropomorphism, the Bible speaks frequently of God looking—to and fro across the earth, at the lights that rule the day and night, at the sea creatures and plants, at us. So it's a perfectly sensible thing for us to do as well, especially while praying, "God be in my eyes—and in my looking."

This week, try it. You might like it.

> *God be in my head*–and in my understanding
> **God be in my eyes–and in my looking** (x10)
> *God be in my mouth*–and in my speaking
> *God be in my heart*–and in my thinking
> *God be at my end*–and at my departing.

Day 12
on a pre-modern take regarding our eyes

The ancient Hebrews, like the pre-moderns behind the Sarum Prayer, didn't have a scientific understanding of the body. All they had was their subjective experience of the body. But a real wisdom comes from this vantage point.

The book of Proverbs refers to the eye as the "window to the soul." This is the experience of looking at someone's eyes. Indeed, our brains are well attuned to discerning another's interior state (fear, wonder, questioning, hostility, mirth, sorrow, boredom) through observing the micro-expressions of the eyes.

Jesus used a different image: "The eye is the lamp of the body" (Matthew 6:22). Not a window letting light in, but a lamp sending light out into the world. To the pre-modern person, the eyes must have felt like headlamps shining light into the surrounding darkness—turn the headlamps off and we're like travelers at night stumbling through a darkness with unseen dangers lurking.

So let's try out this prayer from the vantage point of the two ways our ancient ancestors experienced what eyes can do.

God be in my eyes–and in my looking

That is, *let me see what's going on with the people around me as I look at their eyes, window to the soul. Seeing, let me care.*

God be in my eyes–and in my looking

That is, *when the way forward is obscured by fog or thick darkness, let me find my way with a light you supply from within. Seeing, let me follow.*

Using our meditative format (extra focus on the second line), let us pray with our eyes open,

God be in my head–and in my understanding
God be in my eyes–and in my looking (x10)
God be in my mouth–and in my speaking
God be in my heart–and in my thinking
God be at my end–and at my departing.

Day 13
on feeling more connected to our surroundings

Jill Bolte Taylor was a thirty-seven-year-old neuroanatomist when she had a stroke, which affected the part of her brain that gives us a sense of being separate from our surroundings. Writing in My *Stroke of Insight*, she knew exactly what was going on with her brain, but wasn't prepared for the experience of feeling so deeply connected to everything around her. In fact, as her brain slowly regained the damaged function back, she had to will herself to keep getting better because she didn't want that sense of herself as a "separate-from-surroundings-self" to return.

Hmmm, one thinks. There's a part of our brain responsible for our feeling separate from everything that surrounds us? We don't imagine water molecules feeling separate from the ocean in which they are immersed, and yet we assume that, of course, our sense of separation from our surroundings reflects something fundamental about reality.

Sometimes this separate feeling fades and we feel more deeply connected to our surroundings than usual. We feel absorbed, at times, in nature—standing on the precipice of an expansive vista facing breathtaking beauty. Or we feel one with our choir-mates singing with abandon (and the moment's right). It's always good, this feeling, and we wish for more moments like this.

God be in my eyes–and in my looking

Maybe such moments are conscious-contact-with-God moments. Maybe when we feel this sense of connection we are feeling more like what God feels in relation to us, and the world in which we are immersed.

God be in my eyes–and in my looking

So much of the way our modern lives are organized reinforces our sense of separateness from our surroundings. Perhaps God could be in our eyes, could infuse our looking, in a way that, instead, reinforces our sense of connection.

Let us slow down, take our time, and pray,

God be in my head–and in my understanding
God be in my eyes–and in my looking (x10)
God be in my mouth–and in my speaking
God be in my heart–and in my thinking
God be at my end–and at my departing.

Day 14
on the wonders wrought by looking

A friend (well, OK, my wife), Julia Huttar Bailey, told me of standing watch on her safety patrol corner in Holland, Michigan, when she was ten years old. The lake-effect snow was falling again, another long winter on the West coast of Michigan, with snowing days on end. One morning, Julia noticed a few white snowflakes alight on her navy blue mitten. For the first time, she saw the six-sided crystalline structure of a single snowflake. Some four and a half decades later, Julia told me, dead earnest, her misty eyes bearing witness, "It was a spiritual experience."

The first chapter of the book of Genesis has God making the world in six days. All our English translations show it's a poem, with indentations set to indicate a verse structure. Hebrew poetry relies less on rhyming and more on repetition and structure for poetic effect. Time and again, the placement of the refrain "and God saw that it was good" appears at the end of a stanza for emphasis. We're lulled into a meditative mode by this pattern until the very end, the summing up: "And so it was, and God saw all that he had done, and look, it was very good" (1:31, Robert Alter translation). That "look" is the first appearance of the word, an imperative, in the Bible. While the "saw" in "and God saw that it was good" is an account of God's seeing, this is a command addressed to us, the reader-listener. Until this point, God does all the seeing, as we passively receive the narrator's report. Then God turns toward us to say, "Look!"

When ten-year-old Julia, standing watch on her assigned corner to ensure the safety of her fellow students, saw those few snowflakes alight on her navy blue mitten—their six-sided crystalline structure manifest for the first time in her life in such noticeably bold relief—it was as if God called to Julia, regarding snow, "Look!" And she did look, or rather, God was in her eyes, looking, and she knew something special was happening.

In anticipation of a similar imperative moment coming our way, maybe today, let us pray,

> God be in my head–and In my understanding
> **God be in my eyes–and in my looking** (x10)
> God be in my mouth–and in my speaking
> God be in my heart–and in my thinking
> God be at my end–and at my departing.

Day 15

on the border between two kinds of looking

In an essay titled, "What do I mean to say 'I saw'?" Barbara Newman says the prophets of Israel and others of their time didn't distinguish between what we would call physical seeing and spiritual seeing. So when Isaiah writes "I saw the Lord and his train filled the temple," was he reporting something he perceived by open-eyed sight or was he using the language of the prophet as a "seer," something we would regard as a function of the spiritual imagination? No way to know, says Newman.

Even if we pay lip service to such a thing as "spiritual insight," we automatically assign an unequivocal sense of hard reality to physical sight and a softer, less reliable, less tangible, less significant reality to the other kind. And if we imagine that "spiritual seeing" could be really real, we assume anyone capable of such a thing is an outlier—not at all like us, the sort of people who make up approximately .05 percent of the population.

But what if we paid a little more respect to our pre-modern ancestors, who, as Tanya Luhrmann says (commenting on Newman's essay), "did not tell us whether their images had clear borders or were translucent like a ghost."[2] They didn't because the distinction between the two modes of seeing didn't strike them as all that important. Of course, the realm of spirit peeks out at us from time to time through the thin veil barely separating these intermingling realms, and we, as humans in God's image, can catch occasional glimpses of that other realm. Everyone knows that, no explanations needed. Thus the ancestors of our great-great-great grandparents might have thought.

Out of respect for our elders, we might playfully consider the possibility that they were onto something real. After all, they successfully managed some very harsh realities and lived to pass on their DNA to the likes of us. Maybe we owe them that, at least.

And we have the witness of sacred text to the legitimacy of such things that lie beyond the borders of our conventional wisdom. St. Paul casually employs a phrase in one of his letters, much in keeping with "God be in my eyes—and in my looking." His goes, "the eyes of your heart having been enlightened" (Ephesians 1:18, David Bentley Hart translation). God's light and all that it illumines can be seen by the eyes of our hearts, by which we engage in a real form of looking.

Let us pray, then, today, employing the words of those for whom such things came so easily,

God be in my head–and in my understanding
God be in my eyes–and in my looking (x10)
God be in my mouth–and in my speaking
God be in my heart–and in my thinking
God be at my end–and at my departing.

Day 16

on the desire to be seen

We all want to be noticed. Well, let's refine that. If we're not feeling burned by the wrong kind of attention for the wrong reasons from the wrong people, there are times when we long to be noticed.

This hit me a while back after I'd given a sermon that I wasn't too sure of. It was on privilege in the letter to the Philippians—how Jesus gave his up, and how Paul followed suit. But, you know, privilege, that's a loaded word, no pun intended, plus I was painfully aware that as someone with way more than his fair share of privilege, I was perhaps not one to speak—or at least be listened to on the subject. So I was stopped in my tracks, in a good way, when a congregant I very much respect, and one who didn't share my privileged status, caught me afterwards and said simply, "I see you." This person—almost like a seer or a prophet would—then told me what she saw me doing in the sermon, and this description was everything I would have hoped for, but was so unsure of, given my nagging self-doubt that day. Those three words—I see you—surprised me by the power of their effect on me.

It's a wonderful thing to be seen as your best self by someone whose opinion matters.

So many interactions between Jesus and various individuals were marked by that kind of seeing. Like the way Jesus saw Nathanael under the fig tree, sitting there without any guile, when we have just heard Nathanael say of Jesus, "Can anything good come from Nazareth?" in a snarky, prejudicial way that we know so well because it fits us like a dirty shirt. Jesus saw something in Nathanael—his truest and best self—and in seeing it, brought it more into being.

I would like to be able to see others that way.

Perhaps that would be a fitting desire to affix to this prayer as we pray,

> God be in my head–and in my understanding
> **God be in my eyes–and in my looking** (x10)
> God be in my mouth–and in my speaking
> God be in my heart–and in my thinking
> God be at my end–and at my departing.

5

God be in my mouth—
and in my speaking

Day 17
on being at a loss for words

God be in my mouth–and in my speaking

We're at a loss for words . . . again. What could we possibly say to console our grieving friend after such a crushing loss? Or how do we broach a subject with a loved one that has long terrified both of us, but cries out for attention? Or break the ice with a stranger in hope of making a friend?

What if we can't easily or often or ever seem to find the right words when the right words matter and all the bearing down we do to conjure them only makes it worse?

Perhaps it's time we turn elsewhere than to ourselves for assistance.

God be in my mouth–and in my speaking

This capacity of ours for speech, for uttering an aural code that transplants thoughts from one private mind to another, is a marvel. A wonder. A boundary-expanding spiritual thing if spiritual things are infused among us in our ordinary existence.

Such a deeply spiritual thing that it is fitting to invoke the aid of the deity, the power, the love who brought all things into existence through speaking a word into the silent void.

Maybe we're all like great athletes, or artists, or mechanics, or scientists, who must, from time to time, relax, and trust in a mysterious process of inspiration that unleashes riches we can't simply generate ourselves, but which do, inexplicably, flow through us.

Maybe speaking is more than a skill. Maybe it's a gift we've been given, a gift of our humanity, a reflection of the One whose image we are. That being the case, turning to this Other-than-Ourselves is one of the most sensible and natural things we might do.

Today marks a new week with a new line of the Sarum Prayer. Let's make it our own, as we pray,

> *God be in my head*–and in my understanding
> *God be in my eyes*–and in my looking
> **God be in my mouth**–**and in my speaking** (x10)
> *God be in my heart*–and in my thinking
> *God be at my end*–and at my departing.

Day 18
on overcoming the intimidation factor

The idea of *inspired* speaking, can seem a little over the top, a little beyond our pay grade, so to speak. We could use a little help overcoming the intimidation factor, the one that says, "God be in *my* mouth—and in *my* speaking? You've got to be kidding me." Picturing realities beyond our immediate grasp takes a little imagination. Enter one of the earliest pictures of God interacting with humanity, offered for our consideration in Genesis 2:

> Then the Lord God fashioned the human, humus
> from the soil, and blew into his nostrils the breath
> of life, and the human became a living creature.
> (Genesis 2:7, Alter)

Here's a human we can relate to—in relation to God, a creature of humble origins, if that is not being unfair to dirt (which is pretty amazing stuff on its own). Here's a picture, then, to help us imagine ourselves as divinely connected creatures: God bending over us to infuse us with our first breath.

I don't mean to be too flip here, but put that in your pipe and smoke it. That is, let the Genesis rendering of our first breath affect you. Life is spiritual. You came into the life-realm when The Mystery formed then infused your lungs with air—the first of many in-breaths. Upon entry into this world, we all took (or rather, received) that first breath, and were on our way to speaking, beginning with the primal sputtering and crying of a newborn creature.

Personalize Genesis 2:7—that is, imagine it as a spiritual rendering of your first breath, the one that put you on the road to becoming a communicating being:

> Then the Lord God fashioned *me*, the human, hu-mus from the soil, and blew into *my* nostrils the breath of life, and *I* became a living creature.

"God be in my mouth—and in my speaking" may not be so far-fetched after all.

Attending to the breath that makes life possible, let us pray:

> *God be in my head*–and in my understanding
> *God be in my eyes*–and in my looking
> **God be in my mouth*–and in my speaking** (x10)
> *God be in my heart*–and in my thinking
> *God be at my end*–and at my departing.

Day 19

on singing our way out of a bad mood

It had been a bad word week, humanly speaking. Too many social media clips of people in power spewing ill-advised words, poison words, the kind of speaking that spreads like the flu, and makes you want to stay inside, away from everyone. Thus soured on my species, I nevertheless dragged myself to the Christmas concert featuring folk artists of local, regional, or national renown, gathered to sing their hearts out for us. And they did, mixing and matching in ever-changing arrangements to offer haunting renditions of the human desire for help, salvation, healing—evoking the hope of a resonating higher power eager to respond.

Now and again we all joined in—strangers no longer, the insular borders of ticket-holding cliques dissolving as we formed a choir with these skilled musicians who ushered us into a magical realm. I felt what it must be like to be a bee in a hive buzzing with communal energy, unselfconscious, and only us-aware. Then I saw us all again—we human beings at our best, not our worst—and what it is, what we are, when we image God together.

God be in my mouth–and in my speaking

Sacred speaking in its varied forms is mostly, I wonder, the kind we do with others.

Not so much the quotable comment, the brilliantly uttered insight that sets us apart from the herd, but the laying down of the striving-against-the-others self to speak or sing words written by them, the others, and not ourselves. Words of ancient or newly crafted liturgy, of hymns, old or new, of prayers channeling shared desire for something no one of us can generate or enter alone.

And yes, we did close that concert with "We are the world, we are the children, we are the ones who make a brighter day, so let's start giving," but by then the cynicism, the judgment, the pathetic and entirely unnecessary hostility of Dr. Seuss's Grinch had been removed from me. And yes, some of the words of that pop anthem I couldn't get out for the catch in my throat, and so for those few bars all I could do was listen to the sacred sounds around me.

Aware that we are giving voice to a shared desire, let us pray,

> *God be in my head*–and in my understanding
> *God be in my eyes*–and in my looking
> **God be in my mouth–and in my speaking** (x10)
> *God be in my heart*–and in my thinking
> *God be at my end*–and at my departing.

Day 20
on our limited command of the English language

New Testament translator David Bentley Hart says most English translations of the original *koine* (or common) Greek enhance the literary style of the original text. Paul's Greek, he says, is "generally rough, sometimes inept, and occasionally incoherent." The Gospel of John manages to squeeze its deeply spiritual message out of a Greek that is syntactically (having to do with sentence structure—I had to look it up) "almost childish." The book of Revelation is written in a Greek that is "almost unremittingly atrocious."[3]

Well that's a relief. Apparently, inspired speaking has nothing to do with elegance, erudition, or possession of a whopper vocabulary.

I have a young friend whose speech is affected by cerebral palsy. It can sometimes take a little patience to catch his drift, but he is a deep soul and I have little doubt that God is often in his speaking. Stephen Hawking, the amazing physicist, made use of computer- generated speech for his speaking and the things he said will blow your mind.

Jesus put his finger on it when he said, "Out of the fullness of the heart, the mouth speaks." Our speaking is more to do with our heart than anything. Grammar, vocabulary, nimble manipulation of metaphor and the rest is one thing; God in our mouths speaking, another.

So no, it's not speech class. No sweaty palms required. It's something else entirely, something primal, something basic: "God, be in my mouth—and in my speaking."

Let us muster whatever limited command we have of our native tongue, knowing something more is at work here, and pray,

> *God be in my head*–and in my understanding
> *God be in my eyes*–and in my looking
> **God be in my mouth**–**and in my speaking** (x10)
> *God be in my heart*–and in my thinking
> *God be at my end*–and at my departing.

Day 21
on being prepared to speak a contrary word

Of all the ill-chosen words in scripture, the biggest spotlight shines on Peter's failure of nerve when confronted about his association with Jesus on the night of his betrayal. The scapegoating mechanism had kicked into gear and the crowd dynamic that once made Jesus wildly popular had suddenly gone the other direction to his peril, and Peter's. Peter finds himself on that cold night around a fire, warming his hands with others. "Aren't you with him?" he was asked, and to his deep shame, Peter replied, "No, I never knew the man" followed by the crowing cock. Soon enough, Peter is weeping.

We've all been there. A friend becomes the topic of conversation within the gossipy intimacy of a group of other friends. Observations are made of the absent friend—his boorishness, her insensitivity—and the group congeals deliciously in agreement. We smile or nod in silent assent. At that moment, we cast our glance beyond the circle to see that very friend within earshot and a clear sightline to our concurrence . . . and we feel ashamed.

"In the end, we will remember not the words of our enemies, but the silence of our friends" said Martin Luther

King Jr.—the truth of which we will all come to know as silent friends and the ones betrayed by them.

The thing is we never know when these little circles of false intimacy will form to include us, seducing us, securing in a moment our silent assent. The boldness to speak up with a contravening word will so easily escape us.

There is no turning of crowds against scapegoats, no lynch mobs, no viral-spreading evil, without this mirroring of the group at the expense of the accused member. It is the sin at the foundation of the world, of human society, of every nation, institution, family, wherever two or three are gathered. Meanwhile our tender, obsessive, or calloused consciences are preoccupied with lesser failings.

What we all need is boldness of speech at-the-ready conferred by the indwelling Spirit on the early followers of Jesus in the book of Acts—including our spotlighted representative and leader, the mealy mouthed Simon Peter.

To this end, we are wise to pray, as often as we think to pray,

> *God be in my head*–and in my understanding
> *God be in my eyes*–and in my looking
> **God be in my mouth–and in my speaking** (x10)
> *God be in my heart*–and in my thinking
> *God be at my end*–and at my departing.

Day 22
on the speaking we do inside our heads

Thinking of speaking got me thinking about thinking. What did we do for thinking before we invented language? Which came first, thinking or speaking? Perhaps they arose together among our ancestors in the deep past. Now we do much of our thinking in words that we first learned by hearing them spoken.

Which brings us to some of the most important speaking of all that we do—speaking to ourselves, within ourselves. It's truly mysterious what's going on in us, that more or less constant inner dialogue in which we imagine speaking words that we also imagine hearing—and somehow this adds up to what we call . . . thinking. Whatever this strange phenomenon may be, it is a major stream within our consciousness. It shapes us as surely as flowing water carves a riverbed in rock.

What about this inner speaking—could God be in it? Pray God, be in this speaking!

Today we could ask God to help us notice what we are saying to ourselves within ourselves. What is the tone of our inward speaking? When speaking to ourselves of ourselves and when speaking to ourselves of others? How is this chatter affecting us? What sort of inner paths is our inner speaking carving out in our inner landscapes?

What would it be like to invite God into this realm of our very private speaking? We could try it and see.

> *God be in my head*–and in my understanding
> *God be in my eyes*–and in my looking
> **God be in my mouth–and in my speaking** (x10)
> *God be in my heart*–and in my thinking
> *God be at my end*–and at my departing.

6

※

God be in my heart—
and in my thinking

Day 23
on the thinking heart

No modern prayer would say a thing like "God be in my heart—*and in my **thinking**.*" We do our thinking with our heads and our feeling with our hearts so long as we're not being too literal about it. But there are many ways to slice the pie that is us, many ways to distinguish our various modes of being. "Mind-body-spirit" is an old standby. "Love the Lord your God with all your heart and soul and strength" is another.

Let's give this pre-modern take on a heart that does our thinking for us a chance. The heart is closer to our center of gravity, nestled near our breathing lungs and churning stomachs, like so many dancers on a crowded dance floor, with nerves trundling north to the brain and south to the rest of the body in hope of coordinating the whole. In the human embryo, the heart and the brain arise from an original set of undifferentiated cells, migrating to their respective locations.

The Eastern Orthodox, guarding a tradition that goes back to the desert fathers and mothers praying in Northern Africa, gave us the Jesus Prayer ("Lord Jesus Christ, Son of the Living God, have mercy on me, a sinner," repeated over and over). This meditative practice is thought to induce an experience described by the phrase, "descending with the mind into the heart." The pray-er of the Jesus Prayer would, by means of the prayer, calm their clamoring thoughts, and with a little patience, sense a downward slide of their "center of awareness" from the head, and gradually, into the heart—and by heart here, they mean the beating center located in the chest. Once there, a kind of prayerful thinking would take place—perhaps more visual or affective than word-based thinking, a thinking associated with a different kind of fruitfulness than ordinary cognition.

In a time of over-stimulated and digitally mediated quick thinking—like a split screen with multiple images flashing— this other restful and lollygagging heart thinking sounds appealing, doesn't it?

We could begin by asking,

> *God be in my head*–and in my understanding
> *God be in my eyes*–and in my looking
> *God be in my mouth*–and in my speaking
> **God be in my heart*–and in my thinking** (x10)
> *God be at my end*–and at my departing.

Day 24
on feeling your voice in your chest

The Sarum Prayer invites us out of our cerebral cortex-centered praying, into a kind of praying that inhabits our body as a whole: God be in my head, God be in my eyes, God be in my mouth, God be in my heart.

Whatever heart thinking is (*"God be in my heart*—and in my thinking"), it is slower, less chatter-y, less grinding, and more extra-mentally physical.

Try this, if you're game for it: cross your hands over your chest and pray, "*God be in my heart*—and in my thinking" just loud enough to feel the vibrations of your voice in your chest. It's less important to form the words clearly than to feel your chest vibrating from your voice. Try it for a stretch, a few minutes or so? Tie it to your breathing—in through your nose, then out with "God be in my heart—and in my thinking."

As you pray in this more physically aware way, focus your attention on your body praying less than on your mind praying. As your brain chatters away, let it do so. Keep returning your focus to the feel of your chest vibrating from the words of the prayer. After all, it's a very simple request that doesn't require a lot complicated thinking. It's just asking, "God be in my heart—and in my thinking."

Jesus said, "Ask" using the verb tense that means "keep on asking." So a few minutes of asking is allowed.

This time let your body do the praying, saying,

> *God be in my head*–and in my understanding
> *God be in my eyes*–and in my looking
> *God be in my mouth*–and in my speaking
> ***God be in my heart*–and in my thinking** (x10)
> *God be at my end*–and at my departing.

Day 25
on the heart-thinking of desire

You can imagine how our distant-in-time ancestors would regard the physical heart as the seat of desire, given the way desire can affect the beating of the heart. The heart knows what it wants and tells us. For better or worse and everything in between and beyond, we are desire-driven creatures, made in the image of a desiring God.

Lay aside, for a moment, all suspicion of desire—our guarding against wanting something too much so as not to be disappointed, untangling conflicting desires, feeling captive to desires that seem out of step with our well-being or the well-being of others. All that caution is a given, but it sits alongside our life-honoring desires—for what we need to survive, for passing our genes on, for justice, for meaning, and yes, even for God. It's an untidy thing to be desire-driven creatures, but such is our lot, made, as we are, in the image of a desiring God.

God, the object and subject of ultimate desiring, who desires us—let us leave aside a focus on ourselves, and apply ourselves to praying along these lines:

God be in my heart, seat of my desire–and in my thinking. Take the jumbled, tangled, knotted-up mess of my desires and inhabit the whole desiring heart of mine. Amplify the desires you will, until they expand to fill my heart and leave less space for desires that wouldn't appeal to me if only I knew better.

Tending to the desires of our hearts is a kind of thinking, as Paul, who was as intensely and confusingly a desiring soul as any of us, reveals in this bit of heart-thinking counsel:

Finally, beloved, whatever is true, whatever is honorable, whatever is just, whatever is pure, whatever is pleasing, whatever is commendable, if there is any excellence and if there is anything worthy of praise, think about these things. (Philippians 4:8)

Or, for short, this simpler version, tucked away in the Sarum Prayer,

God be in my head–and in my understanding
God be in my eyes–and in my looking
God be in my mouth–and in my speaking
God be in my heart*–and in my thinking (x10)
God be at my end–and at my departing.

Day 26
on the myth of the heart-head divide

For many centuries, philosophers regarded our rational thinking as a process clearly differentiated from our emotions—hence the thinking-head, feeling-heart division that still holds sway today. Thinking was the higher function, feeling the lower. The religious version of this goes "Put your faith in the facts, and the feelings will follow," as though you could handle your feelings like you curb your dog. It was all very neat and tidy and well-arranged until the neuroscientists discovered that our rational thoughts (our considered moral judgments, for example) are not at all dispassionate in their origins. First comes an intuition (led by finely honed-for-survival emotions and more reactive functions of the brain), then comes a rationale to back up the intuition (led by the rational thinking part of the brain). In others words, before we have what we regard as dispassionate rational thoughts, these thoughts have already been triggered by emotions that we may or may not be aware of.

Thus, locating thinking in the feeling-heart (as this very old prayer does) is not so naïve an idea after all. In fact, it's a very old idea ahead of its time.

And here we are, our minds filled with what we take to be dispassionate/rational thoughts that feel very much like well-considered logical conclusions. In fact, most of these cool-headed perspectives got rolling along their cognitive highway fueled by one or more of our wet, heart-throbbing, sweaty emotions—sad, glad, mad, and all their variant combinations featured in that brilliant animated movie, *Inside Out*. All this happens, of course, in the micro-milli-nanoseconds by which our neurons fire and trigger other neurons to fire.

What can we do about it? For starters, be a little less high-minded about how dispassionate and logical and rational our thinking on a given topic may be. Understand, instead, that every thought is like a passenger on a crowded subway train jostled by emotions of various kinds on every side.

Humility is often a reality-honoring posture. And it leads us to something else we can do about our feeling-thinking: turn to a higher power for a little help with our heart-thinking, which is where our handy fourth line comes in:

God be in my head–and in my understanding
God be in my eyes–and in my looking
God be in my mouth–and in my speaking
God be in my heart–and in my thinking (x10)
God be at my end–and at my departing.

Day 27

on actually finding the word on the tip of your tongue

Have you ever gone to bed, mulling over a problem, and upon waking, the solution pops into consciousness after a strong cup of coffee? I write sermons and I find it helpful to read my sermon notes over on Saturday night, noticing sections that need work—like, "This example is lame, I need a better one." Then I do my final revisions in the early morning, and those noted-the-night-before sections always benefit. There are thinking parts of us that don't fall asleep and work on our behalf during the night shift.

August Kekule is one of the people credited with discovering the circular structure of the benzene molecule (C_6H_6). He reported that while dozing in front of a fire, he dreamt (or daydreamed) of a self-devouring snake alight in the flames—an image that led him to posit the famed benzene ring. There were others at the time suggesting this structure, but the dawning moment, in Kukele's telling at least, happened in a different kind of thinking than our usual cogitation.

We've all been there. Mulling over a problem, searching for an elusive phrase, idea, perspective, or a way to replace that stripped nut on the faucet, we told ourselves, *take a walk, take a shower, take a nap, go to the gym, have a swim, take your mind off it for a spell, and it will come to you.* And it does—often enough.

This, perhaps, is heart-thinking, and why wouldn't it be the kind of thinking to benefit from a divine nudge now and again?

Today if you find your mind grinding away at a problem to no effect other than intensifying frustration, step back, take a relaxing breath or two, and recite our now-familiar Sarum Prayer, pausing to dwell on the quirky fourth line:

> God be in my head–and in my understanding
> God be in my eyes–and in my looking
> God be in my mouth–and in my speaking
> **God be in my heart–and in my thinking** (x10)
> God be at my end–and at my departing.

Day 28
on imagination-malady

Imagination is a form of heart-thinking very much affected by our emotions, attitudes, predispositions, and intentions. Imagination has many avenues of expression, but chief among them is picturing scenarios that help us prepare for the future in advance. Anxiety, worry, fussing over scenarios scripted by our Inner Debbie Downer is a malady of imagination.

Let's assume God has some higher access than we do to the future. How that works, if at all, must necessarily be beyond us, but surely a transcendent God must transcend time, and therefore be present to what we know only as past, present, future.

This would qualify God as a good companion for our heart-thinking regarding the future.

I don't mean spelling the future out for us—though divine intuitions in this regard can't be entirely dismissed. I do mean divine whispers in our head, like a trusted friend saying, "Or maybe not" when we've boarded the train of thought hurtling at break-neck speed to Catastrophe, Pennsylvania. Or like a passenger noticing a driver falling asleep at the wheel, our friend might even bark a sharp "Don't be afraid" to rouse us from our all too familiar fear-dreaming. Or soothe us with a firm "Peace be with you" when we've lost our serenity mojo. Or buck us up with an unexpected "You can do this!" when we've convinced ourselves otherwise.

So if you're way overspent in your fuss-budget, give the fourth line of the Sarum Prayer a little extra time and attention, praying,

> *God be in my head*–and in my understanding
> *God be in my eyes*–and in my looking
> *God be in my mouth*–and in my speaking
> **God be in my heart–and in my thinking** (x10)
> *God be at my end*–and at my departing.

7

~❦~

God be at my end—
and at my departing

Day 29
on facing reality in hope of meeting God there

In pockets of privilege, children can avoid facing death in their circle of family and friends until well into their adult years. Even then, when death finally intrudes, its concrete reality is whisked away like litter at Disneyworld. Until the last hundred years or so, death was a more equal opportunity player. In my middle class Detroit neighborhood, we kindergarteners took a daily rest period to ward off the dreaded poliovirus, and when Jonas Salk came up with his vaccine, we lined up to get our dose (delivered by sugar-cube in a little white cup) as if for a party. All this is mentioned, lest we think the Sarum Prayer's last line is but the bummer end of an otherwise uplifting prayer.

Preparing for life's inevitabilities begins with saying hello to them without plunging into a bad mood. Like the monks do, who daily remove a single shovel full of dirt from what will eventually become their grave. The Lord's Prayer offers an oblique reminder of coming attractions with the petition to "save us from the time of trial." A line in the Psalms opines, "Lord, teach us to number our days that we may love thee with a heart of wisdom." The Book of Common Prayer prompts its daily Compline (or bedtime) users to pray "The Lord Almighty grant us a peaceful night and a perfect end." In a bodily prayer like the Sarum, the day of our death belongs with reference to our head, eyes, mouth, and heart, because all flesh is mortal.

The physical gesture recommended for this final line is to extend open hands. This is a very different gesture than the daily ones we make to acknowledge our mortality—things like buckling our seat belt, watching our sugar intake, or trying, one more time, to stop smoking, all of which are death-avoidance moves. By contrast, open hands signify acceptance: we're all going to die, and we can say so without terror, as much as we can rake leaves or crack an egg for breakfast without plunging into the existential void. Because the real God only meets us in whatever reality we inhabit, mortality being ours.

Let us be alert for God meeting us in our bodies—the real ones, the ones with the expiration date, as we pray:

> *God be in my head*–and in my understanding
> *God be in my eyes*–and in my looking
> *God be in my mouth*–and in my speaking
> *God be in my heart*–and in my thinking
> **God be at my end–and at my departing.** (x10)

Day 30

on the cost of discipleship

The Jesus movement was sparked by someone who thumbed his nose at death. His was not a suicide mission so much as a "do God's will and let the chips fall where they may" mission. Those who become his followers (as opposed to mere adherents) only do so by adopting this attitude. Take, for example, the Reverend Dr. Martin Luther King Jr. Not the commercialized, claimed-by-everyone version, but the real Dr. King whose phones were tapped by the FBI. During his last speech, given at the Church of God in Christ headquarters in Memphis, the day before he was assassinated by a white supremacist, King considered his own death:

> Well, I don't know what will happen now. We've got some difficult days ahead. But it really doesn't matter with me now, because I've been to the mountaintop. And I don't mind. Like anybody, I would like to live a long life; longevity has its place. But I'm not concerned about that now. I just want to do God's will. And He's allowed me to go up to the mountain. And I've looked over. And I've seen the Promised Land.

> I may not get there with you. But I want you to
> know tonight, that we, as a people, will get to
> the Promised Land.[4]

The ninety-nine percent of Christianity-adherents who didn't lift a finger to help their Jewish neighbors during the Nazi era (including an American president who refused sanctuary to a boatload of Jews fleeing persecution) did so out of security fears—loathe to put themselves or their loved ones at increased risk. This is the usual reason we stand by silently while bully-mobs make life miserable for innocent people whose presumed guilt makes them handy scapegoats for our collective and unconfessed sins.

Excuse my bluntness: but following Jesus requires facing death as though it weren't the end of the world. That way, we might be willing to do something more brave than keeping our heads down when vulnerable persons are being put at risk. We might be willing to speak up, say the awkward thing, object, even if it involves some cost to ourselves.

Just because faith is life-affirming in all respects doesn't mean it's death-avoiding at all costs. Jesus, for the joy set before him, endured the cross, despising its shame. King's last public words, immediately following the aforementioned quote, were, "So I'm happy, tonight. I'm not worried about anything. I'm not fearing any man. Mine eyes have seen the glory of the coming of the Lord." Sometimes the fullness of life empowers and calls for a little risk-taking in the short-run.

A prayer that trains us not to freak out at the inevitability of our own death is a good place to start.

> *God be in my head*–and in my understanding
> *God be in my eyes*–and in my looking
> *God be in my mouth*–and in my speaking
> *God be in my heart*–and in my thinking
> **God be at my end**–and at my departing. (x10)

Day 31
on having company for departure day

I was with my mother when she died. Among her last intelligible words were something like, "Look at the flowers outside my window." It was the dead of winter in Michigan, but I looked anyway and saw only the dreary weeks-old snow. She must have had a different "outside my window" in view. Just as her mother, upon dying, said to my father, "Glen, look—the angels!" pointing to the closet, her final words.

You feel pretty helpless attending to someone's dying, especially if you don't want them to die and they do. Yet I was the same help to my mother in her dying as she was to me in my living. I got her things to ease her journey—water to moisten her dry mouth, medicine to ease the pain, and better still, company. The hospice nurse told us that hearing is the last sense to go, so in the hours of her slipping away, we chattered away, hoping the familiar sound of our voices would cheer her.

Company. We're social creatures. It's what we crave.

"God be at my end—and at my departing" is as simple an invitation as "I'm having a birthday party next Wednesday and hope you can come—no gifts, just your company."

God is the Alpha and the Omega, the beginning and the end, and knows to show up. We ask him to come anyway because in the social dance between God and us, it's our part to issue the invitation. Others may be as surprised as we are by the occasion of our departing and find themselves far away from us, or otherwise not able to attend. The Alpha and Omega will be there and we can rest assured.

So we ask away,

> God be in my head–and in my understanding
> God be in my eyes–and in my looking
> God be in my mouth–and in my speaking
> God be in my heart–and in my thinking
> **God be at my end–and at my departing.** (x10)

Day 32
on a possible move to otherwhere

Who wrote this prayer? Don't know and probably never will. Maybe a mother taught it to her children and they adjusted it for theirs. Most prayers, like songs, are informed by other prayers—their words shuffled and reshuffled until one gains sufficient popularity and we have a winner in the survival-of-the-fittest prayer-derby. If the Sarum Prayer were composed no later than the sixteenth century, the original pray-ers would have been well acquainted with grief—life expectancy being roughly thirty-five years, owing to a high infant and childhood mortality.

Out of respect to whomever gave us this prayer, let's pay attention to the words of this final line, the very words and nothing but the words: "God be at my end—and at my departing." Nine words total, four of which refer to death (*my end, my departing*). That sums up the big questions that we never-having-died-before witnesses to death find ourselves pondering. Death is observably an end, but also, perhaps, a departing, a leaving for parts unverified.

I had an old friend who was dying. As a young woman, she had a near-death-experience, the classic variety. Her heart stopped, and she had an awareness of being separated from her body lying on the gurney in the ER, then hovering like a gargoyle in the upper corner of the room, observing hospital personnel working on her body, followed by the tunnel of white light, and the offer from some divine source or "agency of good" to either continue toward the light or return to her body. She chose the latter. Afterwards, she found it impossible to fear death. She was absolutely convinced it was both an end and a departing to a place—one she called, in a final email to me before she died, "otherwhere."

An end calls for a period, full stop, caput. A departing calls for a comma, but in this case one whose following clause is invisible to those of us who have never been there. "Otherwhere" seems to me the perfect designation.

West Side Story has a dying song with the phrase "somewhere, a place for us." Somewhere, nowhere, otherwhere? One can't help but be curious, and a certain playful curiosity is not a bad thing to bring to a prayer like this:

God be in my head–and in my understanding
God be in my eyes–and in my looking
God be in my mouth–and in my speaking
God be in my heart–and in my thinking
God be at my end*–and at my departing. (x10)

Day 33
on entering a cloud of their witness

I've been lucky. Most people I've been with or close to when they are dying haven't been afraid of it. Concerned about how their loved ones will do, yes. Apprehensive about associated suffering, yes (and generally reassured by the kind people involved in hospice care). But distressed about what's next for them? No.

I'm inclined to trust the people who calmly approach the time of their departure with serenity, equanimity, and often, a dose of curiosity. Frequently they have longings to meet loved ones who have gone before them—a kind of excited hope rising up from years of sadness born of absence. All of it seems sacred to me.

What also seems sacred is the many people I know who cultivate a sense of wonder, awe, and delight in this life, despite all the difficult things they experience, despite their fears and bouts of gloom, their loneliness and times of abandonment. I can't help believing that some powerful benevolent goodness surrounds us all, and it peeks in at us from time to time through acts of kindness and moments of surprising beauty.

If pressed, I can make the argument that death is simply God's way of telling us our life is over and not a departing to any otherwhere. But it's just that, an argument. If it's correct, so what? I won't exist to have the glorious feeling of having been proved right.

Instead, I feel drawn to the witness of these dying people I have known. It's very difficult not to trust them, so I've stopped trying. I feel surrounded by a cloud of their witness and I like to enter that cloud when I pray,

> *God be in my head*–and in my understanding
> *God be in my eyes*–and in my looking
> *God be in my mouth*–and in my speaking
> *God be in my heart*–and in my thinking
> **God be at my end**–and at my departing. (x10)

Day 34

on the wonders that lie hidden beneath our feet

As the graveside scenes in so many movies remind us: from dust we came, and to it we return. It's an allusion to the story of Eden and our mythic forebear called in Hebrew, *adam* (not a proper name at this point in the tale, and not yet a gendered being) from *adamah* (dirt-dust-earth). The closest equivalent in English being "human from the humus."

Oh, how we underestimate dirt! My friend Hannah Maria is a biologist in our neighborhood. The other day she asked me to guess how many different species of living creatures were alive in the soil around a particular tree on Hill Street. I knew not to hazard a guess—and awaited her answer. "So far, forty!" she replied, adding, "I've been counting!" She then began to describe various barely visible creatures inhabiting the soil and grass and dead leaves around the tree—called aphids and possibly trilobites and other words that escape me now.

Where I saw only a single tree growing from the ground with some grass and dead leaves at its base, she saw a thriving multi-species community of living creatures. What else am I missing around here?

Life with a capital "L" is a more abundant phenomenon than we can possibly grasp. And if we just step back from our daily preoccupations—the ones that demand the tunneling of our attention—to appreciate its abundance, we begin to see that we are immersed in a thriving, pulsating, ungraspably diverse network, or fabric, or ocean, of life.

Even after we die, our constituent stuff, strictly speaking, doesn't stop participating in life, the humus among us being such an abundant life-incubator.

Even consciousness—the awareness of life as we participate in it—is a group effort, our neurons joined via billions of synaptic connections, and emerging from it all, an awareness we experience, as, for example, the color we call red. Maybe the whole shooting match of living things—life's participating members—is conscious, in an analogous way, of itself, and perhaps, of itself in relation to God. I don't know, I'm just riffing. But it's riffing inspired by the awareness that we can't begin to grasp the abundance of life in which we find ourselves, a realization that Hannah Maria's reported discovery alerted me to.

Don't you get a sense, every now and again, mostly unexpectedly, that things are more wonderful than you can possibly imagine? Perhaps that's a good thing to factor in to our anticipation of the future, including what we—at least from this side of the grave—call dying.

As the preacher said, it may be Saturday, but Sunday's a-comin', so let us pray:

> *God be in my head*–and in my understanding
> *God be in my eyes*–and in my looking
> *God be in my mouth*–and in my speaking
> *God be in my heart*–and in my thinking
> **God be at my end–and at my departing.** (x10)

8

❧

Closing Reflections
on the Sarum Prayer

Day 35
on the effect of praying certain prayers

My wife Julia (the Episcopal priest, did I mention that?) grew up attending a family holiness camp in Mexico, Pennsylvania—a week-long outing in the woods with camp-style holiness meetings in the tradition of the Second Great Awakening that swept much of the country before the Civil War (and I'm happy to report, fueled the abolition movement). She learned a children's song there that goes,

> "Be careful little eyes what you see, be careful
>   little eyes what you see
> For the Father up above is looking down in love,
> So be careful little eyes what you see . . . "

Similar counsel is advised for little mouths and little hands, saying and doing, respectively.

A song like this expects a lot of us, let alone the little children who are taught to sing it.

To me, the finger-wagging "be careful" is nervous-making. The song would reinforce my "Santa Claus Is Coming to Town and I Better Watch Out" side, which would keep me keeping my distance from God, even a watching-from-above loving Father God. It would get me sweating the details on a lot of small stuff and make it likely I'd miss the big stuff—justice, mercy, and staying clear of scapegoating mobs. Which is not to say it couldn't be sung with a different effect, but for me, please don't make me sing that song.

Let's say I grew up singing that song as a kind of prayer and it had the effect I suggest it would in my case. What would I do to relax from the scrupulosity that would make me flinch at the thought of God? I would pray the Sarum Prayer, which is addressed to God, not me. Telling myself "to be careful" and asking God "to be in me" are two very different things. The former puts pressure on me, and the latter doesn't. It's not about avoiding anything so much as not avoiding God. If we can remain invitational toward God, hospitable, welcoming, relaxed-yet-awed-and-respectful, and most of all, unguarded, we'll be better off—that's what this prayer tells me . . . and why I like it so much.

If you like it too, there's no substitute for praying it again and again:

> *God be in my head*–and in my understanding
> *God be in my eyes*–and in my looking
> *God be in my mouth*–and in my speaking
> *God be in my heart*–and in my thinking
> *God be at my end*–and at my departing.

Day 36
on slipping into the mystery of incarnation

"Incarnation" is the teaching that the God of Israel is prone to feel at home in humans, having given us the divine image to carry around. The most repeated phrase in the Sarum Prayer is "God be in my . . . (understanding, looking, speaking, thinking, and at my departing)."

All that sounds a little abstract, like commenting on a poem, prayer, or piece of writing often is. But we're really circling around something that is brazen, raw, and in its own way, sensual. "God be *near* my head" would be intimate enough, but "*in*"?— that's another order of proximity altogether. Sometimes inside my head feels a little fragile and I don't need any bulls running loose in the china shop, so to speak. I hope God is gentle, kind, and careful in there. Maybe a prayer like this prompts us to ask: What kind of God would I *want* to invite into myself? What kind of God could someone like me *survive*?

Thankfully, we don't have to figure this all out, as one might labor over the trigonometry that is one math class beyond our abilities. We don't have to put it into words so it passes muster with whoever we think wields the red pen of theological correction. It's something we learn by absorption, like a child learns a language by hearing it spoken, and imitating what she hears (a pretty effective and amazing process). Patience helps, as does praying the Sarum Prayer, returning to it again and again—a tried-and-true prayer that we use to express ourselves to engage with, and ultimately to undergo God.

With gratitude for these now-familiar words generated by unknown others so long ago, longing for divine company as do we, let us also pray,

God be in my head–and in my understanding
God be in my eyes–and in my looking
God be in my mouth–and in my speaking
God be in my heart–and in my thinking
God be at my end–and at my departing.

Day 37
on learning from our enchanted-world ancestors

Back when this prayer was first used, the world was widely regarded as enchanted—infused with wondrous things at every turn. Ghosts? Angels? Demons? Druids? Various and sundry spirits or spirit phenomena? Par for the course.

Across the English Channel, meanwhile, the Protestant Reformation was raging—against icons, statues of Mary, priests turning wine into blood, and church-authority claims buttressed by tales of saints whose bones cured the sick and whose bodies didn't suffer the normal postmortem decay. The newly invented telescope was debunking supernatural explanations for the lights in the sky and the existence of an angel-and-saint-filled heaven just beyond the reach of the naked eye, up there. The skepticism we have inherited and take for granted was just gaining a foothold within what eventually became a Christianity sorting through the remains of its super-naturalness.

So the people who first prayed "God be in my head, my mouth, my eyes, my heart, and at my departing" had a more settled expectation—that such a thing was not only possible, but likely. Of course God could be in our head, eyes, mouth, heart, affecting us there. Normal, not odd. Nothing to be embarrassed about, nothing to be avoided when talking to one's psychiatrist lest she prescribe something to make it go away.

Imagine a world rife with skepticism that romantic love was anything but a cocktail of hormones and neurotransmitters. We feel such a world licking at our heels even now and it takes a little luster off Valentine's Day. Our modern age has disenchanted our understanding of what it means to be alive in this world.

Every age has its lenses that help us see some things clearly while obscuring other things.

I am not eager to go back to a time when an epileptic seizure was viewed as though it were a scene from *The Exorcist*. Neither am I eager, however, to regard all those pre-modern people as deluded in their experience shot through with mystery and wonder and awe. How it all fits together in some precise balance or "best of both worlds" new synthesis makes my head hurt.

I am willing to open myself to the wonder of a God who can be invoked as the God of the Sarum Prayer is, saying,

> *God be in my head*–and in my understanding
> *God be in my eyes*–and in my looking
> *God be in my mouth*–and in my speaking
> *God be in my heart*–and in my thinking
> *God be at my end*–and at my departing.

Day 38

on retracing Jesus's final days

On the night of his betrayal, Jesus has supper with his disciples, preparing them for what's to come. Ominously, he says a blessing over the bread and wine as though these items on the menu signify the meaning of his impending death, which somehow is "for them."

So much of the focus is on those disciples—their confusion and the mini-drama they have going with Judas, who seems to be peeling off in a dangerous direction. Nevertheless, I find myself thinking about Jesus and how it might have been for him.

As events conspire, he's made his decisions about how to respond, and now he's undergoing what amounts to a big test, a trial. A wave is washing over him and where it will take him remains to be seen. If you've had some sudden turn of events overtake you—an unexpected death in your family, a job loss, a deployment notice during wartime, a really bad diagnosis—you know the feeling. It's not the time to prepare so much as to lean into whatever preparations you've already made.

Jesus didn't pray the Sarum Prayer *per se,* but his understanding of God, and himself in relation to God, was very much in line with it. Jesus knew a God who was happy to dwell in him, as the Gospel of John emphasizes. Jesus used language like "God in me and me in God and we are altogether" (a very rough paraphrase). I don't think Jesus was necessarily born with this understanding. I think he arrived at it as we arrive at any understanding—gradually, in fits and starts, by experience and reflection on experience. And now, as this test grinds on, he will soon discover how his bet pays off. We're all betting on something—and time will prove it out.

This prayer is our gamble on God:

> *God be in my head*–and in my understanding
> *God be in my eyes*–and in my looking
> *God be in my mouth*–and in my speaking
> *God be in my heart*–and in my thinking
> *God be at my end*–and at my departing.

Day 39
on being, please

Good Friday, pshaw. Nothing good about it for the one to whom it happened, when it was happening anyway. "Blessed in the eyes of the Lord is the death of his saints," strains credulity in this case. Let's call it a worst-case-death scenario especially in the context of imagining our own. By contrast, may we all slip away gently into that good night.

I can't make any sense of Jesus' death if I think of him in his divine nature. All that seems so remotely theoretical at the point of death, so impossibly complicated to square with "who being in very nature, God." So I just go with the fully human Jesus suffering for those hours. And no, I'm not planning to pound it into our heads—how bad it was—as if this is the Mel Gibson movie.

It seems he felt intensely at his death what we feel vaguely and intermittently through our lives: possibly abandoned by God and possibly near God. All of which I find oddly consoling. His experience—this person I admire beyond words—and mine, have something in common. I feel sometimes abandoned, sometimes connected, and often just focused on slaking a thirst or shifting position to get more comfortable.

I can't imagine my own death except to take a stab in the dark, one that by probabilities alone is almost certainly wrong, but I can imagine his, having heard so much about it. Having celebrated it, in fact. Having pondered it through eating bread and drinking wine with others.

His abject vulnerability in dying reminds me how I feel sometimes, without the spotlight of history on me as it was, apparently, on him. In those moments, all the other words of the Sarum Prayer fade, and the ones that mean the most to me, the ones I feel with greatest longing, are "God be." Please, let a God like this man seemed to know, seemed to express, seemed to represent, seemed to believe in, seemed to hope for, be.

And so, in remembrance of his good Friday, I pray,

God, be.
God, be.
God, be.
God, be.
God, be.

Day 40
on giving God, and ourselves, a rest from our praying

Whenever Easter rolls around, we tend to think of "Holy Saturday" as a day without focus. This probably belies our non-Jewishness, and the eclipse of a seventh day Sabbath in most of Christianity, once Gentiles took over the church. Yet there it is, preserved by the Jewish people to this day: Sabbath.

Sabbath-rest is much more than a cessation of labor. The rest of Sabbath, going back to the original seventh day of creation in Genesis 1, means to "descend upon, fill, inhabit, dwell"—as God, having completed the construction of the earth in six days, came to fill it with divine presence on the seventh. This is the rest of Isaiah's vision: "I saw the Lord! And his train filled the temple!" The Sabbath has always been the day of fullness for Israel, the day of joy that forbids work as a distraction from this other, main event. Sabbath is the day of no more asking, no more longing, no more laboring, but a day to enjoy God filling his temple—everything around us, including us.

For the previous thirty-nine days, we have been praying the Sarum Prayer, which involves a kind of asking. Every sentence in English needs a verb, an action word, without which it is incomplete. The Sarum Prayer verb (the only one) is the subtle-action word "be"—"God *be* in my head, eyes, mouth, heart, and at my end." Be, as in exist, dwell, inhabit, and yes, rest.

As long as we're in the grammar weeds, verbs also have something called moods that shade their meaning. The imperative mood indicates command. If "God be in my head" were in the imperative mood, the meaning would be "God, I'm telling you, be in my head!" In the case of the verb "be," context and speaker intention affect mood. So, we could pray "God be in my head" in the imperative mood—children, after all, do make demands on parents and it's not without precedent in Israel's sacred stories. More likely, we would pray in what my English professor friend tells me is the optative mood, used to indicate a wish or hope. I'll bet most of us have been praying the Sarum Prayer in the optative mood these past thirty-nine days.

Today, let us replace this word "be" with another word more in keeping with the understanding of Sabbath as a day to enjoy, as a day to commemorate God's resting among us, filling the earth with divine presence.

Today, no asking, no longing, no wishing, no hoping.

Today let's give God, and ourselves, a rest from our praying. All it takes is replacing the action word "be" with the even more subtle action word "is." This transforms the

Sarum Prayer into the Sarum Confession: "God *is* in my head, etc."

To the extent that God seems (to you) not yet to be in your head, eyes, mouth, and heart—ignore that, and focus on the extent to which God *must be there already* (for in God we live and move and have our being). Muster a mustard seed of conviction, then, along with a little gratitude, to confess:

> *God is in my head*–and in my understanding
> *God is in my eyes*–and in my looking
> *God is in my mouth*–and in my speaking
> *God is in my heart*–and in my thinking
> *God is at my end*–and at my departing.

Endnotes

1   *Twelve Steps and Twelve Traditions* (New York: Alcoholics Anonymous World Services 2002), 8.

2   T.M. Luhrmann, *When God Talks Back: Understanding the American Evangelical Relationship with God* (New York: Alfred A. Knopf, 2012), 248.

3   David Bentley Hart, *The New Testament: A Translation* (New Haven, CT: Yale University Press, 2017), xxi–xxii.

4   Martin Luther King Jr, *A Testament of Hope*, ed. James Melvin Washington (New York: Harper One, 1991), 286.